Art Projects
from Around the World

Grades 1–3

by Linda Evans, Karen Backus, and Mary Thompson

NEW YORK • TORONTO • LONDON • AUCKLAND • SYDNEY

MEXICO CITY • NEW DELHI • HONG KONG • BUENOS AIRES

Teaching *Resources*

This book is dedicated to artists from around
the world whose creativity and skills have inspired us
to share art from other cultures with our students.

Project introductions edited by Catherine M. Tamblyn

Cover design by Jason Robinson

Cover and interior photography by Studio 10

Interior illustrations by Cary Pillo

Interior design by Sydney Wright

ISBN: 0-439-38531-8
Copyright © 2006 by Linda Evans, Karen Backus, and Mary Thompson
Published by Scholastic Inc.
All rights reserved.
Printed in the U.S.A.

8 9 10   40   13 12

Contents

Introduction

Take a trip around the world with 20 unique art projects that connect to different countries! Some of the projects are based on an art form or craft from a particular culture. Other projects are inspired by a country's geography, history, or culture. You'll find woven paper kente cloth from Ghana, 3-D tree frogs from the rain forests of Brazil, flower paintings from Japan, and much more. The projects are designed to tie in to your curriculum and help students meet the social studies, geography, and visual arts standards.

The projects in this book are easy to create and use readily accessible materials. Each project includes:

◆ background information explaining how the project connects to the country of origin.

◆ illustrated, step-by-step directions.

◆ a materials list.

◆ recommended resources, such as books and Web sites.

◆ color photo of a sample project (see insert).

Creating multicultural art projects provides a hands-on way for students to learn about countries around the world as well as develop an appreciation of and respect for different cultures. We hope you and your students enjoy the journey!

Connections to the Standards

The activities in this book connect to the following standards and benchmarks outlined by Mid-continent Research for Education and Learning (McREL), a nationally recognized nonprofit organization that collects and synthesizes national and state K–12 standards.

Social Studies

—Understands various meanings of social group, general implications of group membership, and different ways that groups function:
- Knows that language, stories, folktales, music, and artistic creations are expressions of culture

—Understands the folklore and other cultural contributions from various regions of the United States and how they helped to form a national heritage:
- Understands how arts, crafts, music, and language of people from a variety of regions influenced the nation

—Understands selected attributes and historical developments of societies in Africa, the Americas, Asia, and Europe:
- Understands the daily life, history, and beliefs of a country as reflected in dance, music, or other art forms (such as paintings, sculptures, and masks)

Geography

—Understands the characteristics and uses of maps, globes, and other geographic tools and techniques

—Knows the location of places, geographic features, and patterns of the environment

—Understands the physical and human characteristics of place

—Understands concepts of region

—Understands the nature and complexity of Earth's cultural mosaics

Visual Arts

—Understands and applies media, techniques, and processes related to the visual arts

—Knows how to use structures (e.g., sensory qualities, organizational principles, expressive features) and functions of art

—Knows a range of subject matter, symbols, and potential ideas in the visual arts

—Understands the characteristics and merits of one's own artwork and the artwork of others

—Understands the visual arts in relation to history and cultures:
- Knows that the visual arts have both a history and a specific relationship to various cultures
- Identifies specific works of art as belonging to particular cultures, times, and places
- Knows how history, culture, and the visual arts can influence each other

---

Source: *Content Knowledge: A Compendium of Standards and Benchmarks for K–12 Education*, 4th Edition (Mid-continent Research for Education and Learning, 2006).

How to Use This Book

The projects in this book are designed for flexible use. You can connect projects to topics in your social studies curriculum or use them on their own. Below are suggestions for making the most out of the learning experience.

Preparation

◆ In advance, review the background information and find photographs for students to use as reference or for inspiration. (Recommended books and Web sites are printed on the project pages.)

◆ Review the instructions, and create a sample project to show students.

◆ Gather the materials, and cut paper or other supplies to the size specified for the activity.

◆ Prepare the work space. For projects that involve painting or messy materials, cover tables with newspaper and have students wear smocks.

Introducing the Project

◆ Before students begin a project, point out the country on a map and present students with information about the country.

◆ Describe the project and explain how the project connects to the culture of that country. You'll find background information, Web sites, and recommended books on each project page.

◆ Show students photographs that connect to the project. Look for examples in books, magazine articles, travel brochures, and online. Museum Web sites are an excellent source of quality images. If a project is based on a form of art, show photographs of the art form or bring in samples, if possible.

Cultural Sensitivity Note
Some of the projects in this book connect to topics with deep spiritual significance for native cultures. Please impress upon your students that these projects are intended to help them learn about these cultures and develop respect and appreciation for them.

Celebrate Cultures!

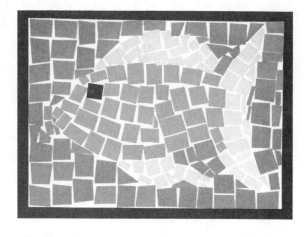

Here are additional ideas to immerse students in cultural studies:

- Create a bulletin board with maps, photos, postcards, travel brochures, and other information about a particular country.

- Play music from a particular country while students work on their projects.

- Invite people from different countries (or people who have traveled to different countries) to your classroom to share information and photos with students.

- Have students share information about their own heritage. Encourage them to talk to family members about where they or their ancestors are from.

- Plan a trip to a local museum so that students can view authentic cultural artwork.

- Have students research different aspects of the countries you have studied, such as arts and crafts, geography, history, and cultural groups.

Art Tips

- If a project involves painting or glue, plan in advance where you will place the projects to dry.

- If students are eager to begin before you have finished giving directions, distribute the art supplies after you have explained each step.

- Put tempera paint on foam trays or paper plates for easy cleanup.

- To clean tempera paint off paintbrushes, soak the brushes for ten minutes in water with a little dishwashing soap. The paint will rinse off quickly.

Display Tips

- For a simple way to mount a painting or drawing, give students sheets of paper that have been trimmed an inch on each side. For example, cut 12- by 18-inch paper so that it's 11 by 17 inches. You can then glue the painting or drawing onto a larger sheet of paper in a different color to create a border.

- To unify your displays, use large background paper or fabrics with cultural motifs that connect to the country of origin.

- In your displays, include information about the countries and the projects. Describe how the projects were created and how they connect to particular countries.

Woven Paper Kente Cloth

Students weave paper into a pattern to resemble colorful kente cloth.

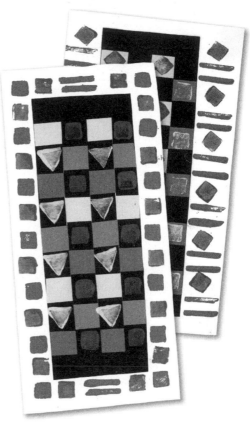

Kente cloth is a colorful patterned fabric traditionally made by the Ashanti (or Asante) people of Ghana. Large pieces of the cloth are made from long, narrow strips of silk, rayon, or cotton, which are sewn together. Geometric shapes and patterns are repeated in the weavings and are combined with distinct decorative techniques. Gold, red, black, and green are the colors most often featured.

The origin of this textile is linked to a popular legend. It tells the story of a weaver who learned his skill by studying a spider weave its web. Once worn only by kings, kente cloth is now sought and worn by people around the globe. Kente cloth is considered special by the Ashanti and worn only on important occasions. This elaborate fabric continues to play a vital role in the Ashanti culture.

Getting Started

Place newspaper on tables and prepare the work space for painting. Pour the paints on paper plates in a thin layer. Divide the class into groups. Provide each group with three plates of paint and a set of wood or foam shapes for printing. Have students wear smocks for this project.

Point out Ghana on a map and review the above information with students. Show them photographs or samples of kente cloth for inspiration. Demonstrate the steps as students follow along.

Materials

- photographs or samples of kente cloth
- 4- by 12-inch black paper
- pencils
- rulers
- scissors
- 1- by 5-inch red, yellow, and green paper (several strips per student)
- glue sticks
- 6- by 14-inch white paper
- red, yellow, and green paint
- paper plates
- wood or foam shapes, such as circles, squares, and triangles, sized to fit on woven paper strips

Resources

For Teachers

African Textiles by John Gillow (Chronicle, 2003). This survey of textiles from different parts of Africa features hundreds of color photographs and illustrations.

Culture and Customs of Ghana by Steven J. Salm and Toyin Falola (Greenwood, 2002). A cultural overview of Ghana.

Wrapped in Pride: Ghanaian Kente and African American Identity by Doran H. Ross, et al. (UCLA, 1998). Explores the history of kente cloth.

For Students

Ashanti to Zulu: African Traditions by Margaret Musgrove (Dial, 1976). Celebrations, ceremonies, and the traditions of 26 African peoples are explored. Includes a page about kente cloth. The colorful and highly detailed illustrations earned the Caldecott Medal for illustration team Leo and Diane Dillon.

Kente Colors by Deborah M. Newton Chocolate (Walker Books for Young Readers, 1997). The simple text explains the importance of kente cloth to several peoples of Ghana and Togo, while the lush illustrations allow students to absorb the richness of these celebrations.

Directions

1 Fold the black paper in half so that the four-inch edges touch. On the folded edge, use a pencil and ruler to draw a line one inch from the edge of the paper.

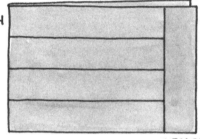

2 Starting from the fold, use a pencil and ruler to draw three horizontal lines that are each one inch apart. Stop at the line drawn in step 1.

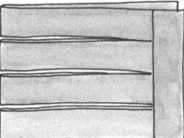

3 Cut along each line, starting at the fold and stopping at the line drawn in step 1.

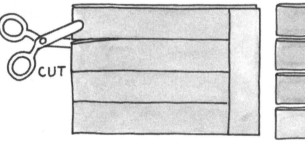

4 Open the paper. Explain to students that these strips represent the warp threads. The paper strips that they will weave over and under represent the weft threads. (Hold the paper vertically to match the direction of warp threads on a loom.)

WARP THREADS

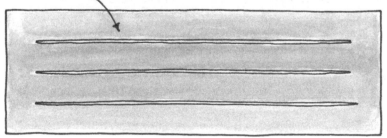

5 Choose several colored paper strips to create a pattern (for example, yellow, green, red, yellow, green, red). Begin on either the left or right side of the page, weaving the first strip over the first warp strip and under the second one. Continue until the entire weft strip is woven.

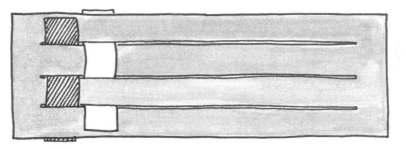

WEFT THREADS

6 Choose a different-colored paper strip. This time, weave it under the first warp strip and over the second one.

7 Continue until the page is completed. Glue the edges of the strips in place.

8 Glue the page onto the center of the white paper to create a frame. Dip the stamps into small amounts of paint and print patterns on the strips and on the frame. Lay flat to dry.

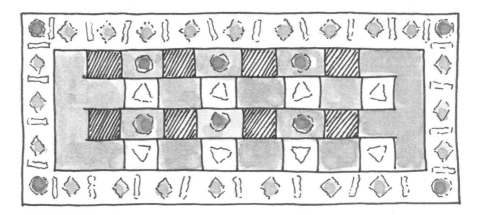

More Ideas

◈ Cover the completed projects with contact paper and use them for holiday place mats.

◈ Use yarn and fabric scraps to weave colorful wall hangings.

Painted Masks

Students paint oversized masks inspired by traditional masks from Burkina Faso.

Masks from Burkina Faso and neighboring West African countries are often carved from wood and are decorated with materials such as fur, leather, natural fibers, pigment, and shells. The facial characteristics of the masks depict humans, animals, or a combination of human and animal features. Some are painted with geometric designs. Varieties include plank masks, helmet masks, face masks, forehead masks, headdress masks, and shoulder masks. The masks in this activity are inspired by the face masks and costumes created by the Winiama, Mossi, and Nuna of Burkina Faso.

For many centuries, masks have played major roles in the rituals, celebrations, funerals, ceremonial initiations, and other practices of different cultural groups. The masks often represent supernatural powers, such as departed ancestors and spirits of the natural world. Mask wearers are chosen or initiated dancers. It is believed that the spirit of the ancestor possesses the wearer of the mask. Full body ceremonial attire is commonly worn with masks. Rituals and ceremonies are accompanied by music, movement, and dance to express social, moral, and religious values of the cultural groups.

Getting Started

Place newspaper on tables and prepare the work space for painting. Have students wear smocks for this project.

Point out Burkina Faso on a map. Review the above information about African masks. Discuss the traditional masks from Burkina Faso. Show students photographs or samples of the masks. Discuss the use of materials and note the stylized aspects. Demonstrate the steps as students follow along.

Materials

- photographs or samples of masks from Burkina Faso
- sketch paper
- pencils
- 12- by 18-inch heavy tagboard
- brown, gray, tan, orange, red, black, and white tempera paint
- small, medium, and large paintbrushes
- scissors
- hole punch
- raffia

Sensitivity Note
This project connects to a topic that holds deep spiritual significance for native cultures. Please impress upon your students that the project is intended to help them learn about these cultures and develop respect and appreciation for them.

Directions

1 On sketch paper, plan your mask shape and draw facial features. Have students use the photographs for reference as they sketch several small mask designs.

2 Choose one design. Use a pencil to enlarge the design on a sheet of tagboard. Guide students to make their masks symmetrical. Paint the facial features on the mask.

3 Use a large brush to paint the large areas of the mask, making sure to paint each side the same. Let the paint dry. (Note: It is easier to paint large areas of color and add the design details of top after the paint is dry, rather than paint around the details.)

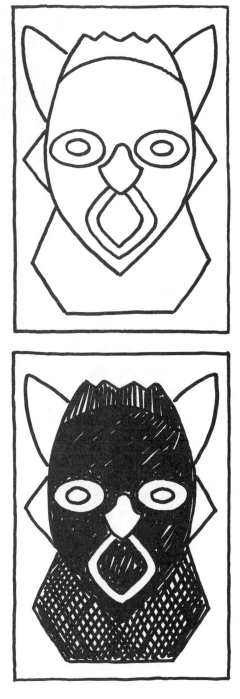

4 Once the paint is dry, use smaller brushes to add details such as lines or dots. Let the paint dry.

Resources

For Teachers

African Masks by Iris
Hahner-Herzog (Prestel,
1998). Includes essays and
nearly 250 photos of
African masks found in the
Barbier-Mueller Collection.

*The Art of African Masks:
Exploring Cultural Traditions*
by Carol Finley (Lerner,
1999). Examines the
traditional use of African
masks, how they are
made, and the significance
of their creation to the
cultures in which they were
developed. Appropriate
for older students.

For Students

*Can You Spot the Leopard?
African Masks* by Christine
Stelzig (Prestel, 1997).
This book for older
students explores the
significance of decorative
elements, particularly the
representation of animals,
in the masks of a variety
of African peoples.

5 Cut out the
finished mask.
Use a hole punch
to punch holes
along the top,
sides, or bottom.
Tie raffia pieces
in each hole.

More Ideas

❖ Discuss the artist Pablo Picasso and how his paintings and
sculptures were influenced by African art.

❖ Study masks from other places, such as Mexico, Alaska,
Indonesia, or China.

❖ For an oval mask, cut a 2-inch slit at the top of the mask,
overlap the pieces, and tape them together to give the mask
a three-dimensional look. Cut another slit at the bottom of
the mask, overlap the pieces, and tape them together.

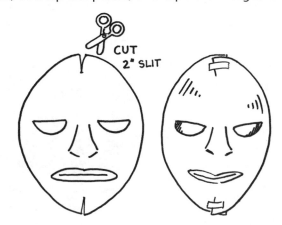

❖ Display the masks by stapling them to sheets of 12- by 18-inch
black paper.

Paper Lion Heads

The "king of beasts" will inspire students to create a cut-paper lion head.

The grasslands in Kenya's National Park, Masai Mara, are home to wildlife such as the elephant, antelope, zebra, jackal, giraffe, and—the "king of beasts"—the powerful lion. Lions have short coats of tawny brown. Most males have brown or black shaggy manes of varying length. The mane covers the head, except the face, and the neck down to the shoulders and chest. Female lions, or lionesses, lack manes.

Lions live in family groups called prides. Prides vary in composition but may contain up to 40 members. Prides usually consist of a single adult male and about six adult females, along with their offspring. The main responsibility of mature males is to protect the pride. Lionesses do most of the hunting, often in teams. Competition from humans for grassland has led to a drastic reduction of the lions' habitat. In addition to living on grasslands, some lions live in the Kalahari Desert of southern Africa.

Getting Started

Point out Kenya on a map. Review the above information with students. Show them photographs of lions and discuss their facial features. Have students use these photographs for reference as they create their projects. Then demonstrate the steps as students follow along.

Materials

- photographs of lions
- scissors
- glue
- 12- by 18-inch brown construction paper (or open and cut a large brown paper bag to size)
- 2- by 3-inch yellow, orange, brown, and tan construction paper (5–6 per student)
- 9- by 12-inch yellow, tan, and brown, construction paper (several per student)
- 6- by 9-inch tan construction paper
- 2-inch squares of black construction paper
- 3-inch thin yellow foam or felt circle
- black markers
- paper straws or brown or black pipe cleaners, cut to 3–4 inches (6 per student)

Resources

For Teachers

An African Experience: Wildlife Art and Adventure in Kenya by Simon Combes (Clive Holloway Books, 1994). A beautifully illustrated travelogue.

Mara-Serengeti: A Photographer's Paradise by Jonathan Scott and Angela Scott (Voyageur, 2001). Features more than 200 stunning color photographs of the Masai Mara and the Serengeti.

For Students

The African Cats by Geoffrey C. Saign (Franklin Watts, 1999). Describes ten African cats, including the lion, cheetah, and leopard. Although this book is written for older students, younger children will enjoy the colorful photos.

Honey . . . Honey . . . Lion! A Story From Africa by Jan Brett (Putnam, 2005). In this retelling of the African fable, Honeybird seeks revenge by fooling a greedy badger into a lion's lair. This beautifully illustrated tale makes an excellent read-aloud. A summary page lists the animals and their names.

Kenya, Jambo! by Katherine Perrow Klyce (Redbird Press, 1989). This book and CD set provides an informative introduction to daily life in Kenya.

Directions

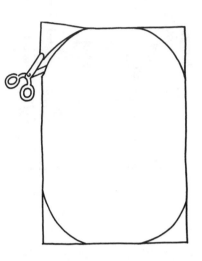

1 Position a sheet of 12- by 18-inch brown construction paper vertically. Use scissors to round off the corners to form a large oval for the lion's head. (At this point, have students write their name on the back.)

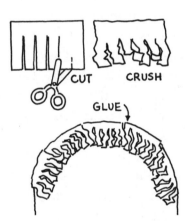

2 Choose several colors of 2- by 3-inch papers. Cut a fringe along the three-inch edge. Then crush the fringes in your hand. Glue five or six pieces along the top of the oval (with the fringe pointing to the head) to form the top part of the mane.

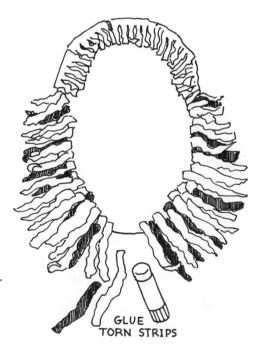

3 Choose several colors of 9- by 12-inch papers and tear them into strips for the lower mane. (Note: Tear the paper along the grain to avoid ripping the paper into small chunks.) Glue approximately 20 to 30 of these strips along the lower face, overlapping them to create a full mane.

4 Fold the 6- by 9-inch tan paper in half width-wise (like a book). On one side, draw an outline of a large ear. Beside the ear, draw an outline of a large eye. Cut out the eyes and ears.

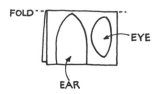

5 Fold the bottom edge of the ears to create a tab. Glue the tab onto the top of the lion's head so that the ears stand up. Glue on the eyes.

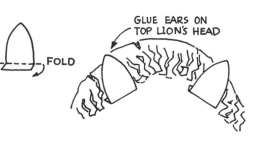

6 Draw and cut a nose from the black paper. Cut out two pupils for the eyes from the scraps. Glue on the nose and pupils.

7 Cut the foam or felt circle in half. Use the marker to draw several dots on each half. Glue the half circles under the nose, at a slight angle.

8 Use the marker to draw a letter J for half the mouth. Draw a backward J to finish the mouth.

9 Glue three straws or pipe cleaners onto each half circle for whiskers.

More Ideas

◆ To make the lion head three-dimensional, glue a second oval to the back of the head. Glue around the edges, leaving a small section open at the top for adding stuffing. Let dry, and stuff with crushed paper towels or newspaper. Glue the opening closed.

◆ Invite students to write a story about going on a safari and observing their lion. Or have students write their story from the lion's perspective.

Cat Portraits

Students paint a fanciful feline after learning about Bastet, the cat goddess.

Many of ancient Egypt's finest works of art were produced for tombs and temples. A favorite subject of ancient artisans was the cat. Excavated artifacts such as bracelets, amulets, and statuettes bear the likeness of felines. Tomb paintings reveal cats as part of daily Egyptian home life. Early records tell us that cats were valued protectors of food in homes and in granaries.

The ancient Egyptians held cats sacred and protected them by law. Cats were seen as embodiments of the goddess Bastet, who was portrayed as a woman with the head of a cat. Bastet was the bringer of good fortune and health. She was believed to be the protector of women, children, and cats. The ancient Egyptians treated cats with great care and respect. They often adorned cats with jewelry and mummified them in the same way as humans.

Getting Started

Place newspaper on tables and prepare the work space for painting. Have students wear smocks for this project.

Point out Egypt on a map. Review the above information with students. Show them photographs of Egyptian art and discuss some of its characteristics. Then demonstrate the steps as students follow along.

Materials

- photographs of Egyptian art
- 9- by 12-inch white drawing paper
- pencils
- crayons
- watercolor paint
- watercolor brushes
- water containers
- sequins
- glue
- 12- by 15-inch colored construction paper

Directions

1 On the white paper, draw an outline of a cat with pencil.

2 Draw line designs on the cat's body.

3 Use a crayon to go over the pencil lines, pressing heavily.

4 Use a crayon to draw patterns and designs in the background.

5 Paint the area around the cat with watercolor paints. Select a different color and paint the cat. (Note: The watercolor may be painted on top of the crayon. If the crayon lines are pressed heavily, the crayon will resist the paint and show through.) Let dry.

6 Glue on sequins to add jewelry to your cat.

7 Place the cat picture in the center of a sheet of 12- by 15-inch paper to create a frame. Glue in place.

More Ideas

❖ To create a double frame, as shown in the sample project, use two sizes of colored paper that are larger than 9 by 12 inches. Glue one on top of the other and glue the cat painting in the center. Experiment with different colors of frames to determine which colors complement the colors in the painting.

❖ Choose other types of Egyptian art to inspire art projects. For example, have students draw figures standing in the Egyptian stance with torso facing forward and face in profile.

Resources

For Teachers

The Art of Ancient Egypt by Gay Robbins (Harvard University Press, 2000). A comprehensive study of art in ancient Egypt

PBS: Egypt's Golden Empire
http://www.pbs.org/empires/egypt
Includes information about life in ancient Egypt.

For Students

Cat Mummies by Kelly Trumble (Clarion, 1996). Written for older students, this book about the role of cats in ancient Egypt makes a delightful and informative read-aloud.

Egypt (Scholastic History Readers) by Stephen Krensky (Scholastic, 2002). Explores different aspects of daily life in ancient Egypt.

Ms. Frizzle's Adventures: Ancient Egypt by Joanna Cole (Scholastic, 2001). Ms. Frizzle and gang travel to ancient Egypt.

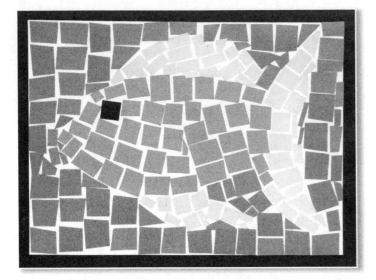

Paper Mosaics

This paper project introduces students to the ancient art of mosaic tile decoration.

Mosaics are designs or story pictures created with small pieces of broken tile, glass, marble, wood, or other materials that are affixed to a surface. The space between the tiles is filled with mortar. By arranging light colors against dark backgrounds or by outlining shapes with black tiles, mosaic artisans can make pictures stand out with limited color combinations.

Mosaic art has a long history in the Middle East and Europe. Mosaics decorate floors, ceilings, walls, and exterior surfaces. Archaeologists in Israel have unearthed numerous mosaics in ancient ruins of homes, churches, and synagogues. These mosaics depict a variety of subjects including astrological signs of the zodiac, Jewish religious symbols such as the Torah and menorah, and other objects with religious significance such as stars. These ancient mosaics have enabled archaeologists to learn about the people who lived in this part of the world throughout the ages.

Getting Started

As you are preparing the paper squares, place them in trays by color. (If desired, provide students with 1- by 12-inch strips of paper and scissors and have them cut the strips into 1-inch squares as part of the project.)

Materials

- photographs of mosaic tile art
- 1-inch squares of colored construction paper (approximately 100 squares per student)
- trays (1 per color of paper)
- 9- by 12-inch white paper
- pencils
- scissors
- glue
- 11- by 14-inch black construction paper

Point out Israel on a map. Show students several photographs of mosaic tile art and review the information on page 18 with them. Discuss how the artists used the small squares of stone tiles in various colors to create a larger picture. Explain to students that the tiles are called tesserae. The white area between the tiles is called mortar. Demonstrate the steps as students follow along.

Directions

1 Use pencil to draw a simple picture (animals or flowers work well). Explain to students that they should use large shapes to create their drawing and try to fill the page.

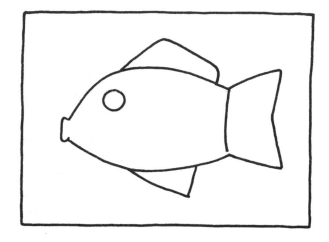

2 Plan the colors of the "tiles" that you will use for your mosaic. You might place them on the drawing before gluing them in place, to see how they look.

3 Fill in the inside of the drawing with paper squares, gluing on a small section at a time. To fill in small spaces, cut the squares to fit. Remind students to leave small spaces between the squares to represent the mortar.

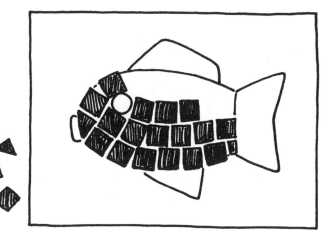

Resources

For Teachers

Ancient Mosaics by Roger Ling (Princeton University Press, 1998). A survey of mosaics in the Greco-Roman world.

Classic Mosaic: Designs and Projects Inspired by 6,000 Years of Mosaic Art by Elaine M. Goodwin (Trafalgar Square, 2000). A respected mosaic artist explains how a mosaic is developed from design into a finished piece. Includes classically inspired project designs.

Making Mosaics: Designs, Techniques, and Projects by Leslie Dierks (Sterling, 1997). Step-by-step illustrations for 12 mosaic projects.

For Students

Count Your Way Through Israel by James Haskins (Carolrhoda, 1992). This book connects the Hebrew numbers 1 through 10 to topics about the history, geography, and culture of Israel.

4 Continue to fill the shape, using several colors to create the design.

5 Choose a contrasting color to fill the area around the picture. Glue on the squares, again leaving a small amount of space between them.

6 Glue the completed mosaic in the center of a sheet of black construction paper.

More Ideas

❖ Display the finished tiles close together on the wall, to simulate an ancient mosaic wall.

❖ Have students create mosaics using one-inch squares of colorful patterns cut from old magazines. They might use these in addition to or instead of construction paper squares.

❖ Have students arrange the completed mosaics to tell a story. Place the mosaics on the floor so that students can see them. Have the first student choose a mosaic and start a story using the mosaic as inspiration. Have the next student choose a different mosaic and continue the story. (As each student takes a turn, display the mosaics in order on a wall.) Continue until all the mosaics have been used or until the story is resolved.

❖ Invite students to create several mosaics illustrating the growth of a plant or other steps in a succession of events.

Good Luck Elephants

Students create a paper collage of an elephant decorated for an Indian festival.

Asian elephants, also known as Indian elephants, are among the largest and most powerful of all living land mammals. Asian elephants are smaller than their African counterpart. They are gentle and live in peaceful family units, usually made up of two to twenty females and their offspring. Full-grown males are solitary. Asian elephants are found in the jungles of India as well as Cambodia, China, Indonesia, Malaysia, Myanmar, Sri Lanka, Thailand, and Vietnam.

Asian elephants are highly intelligent and can be trained to work and perform. Many Asian elephants work in India's logging industry. Their immense strength allows them to move downed trees and brush. The Asian elephant is also an integral part of India's cultural history. It is considered a good luck symbol. Many tamed elephants are kept in temples. On festival days and for processions and parades, elephants are decorated with painted designs, jewelry, and fancy blankets.

Getting Started

Point out India on a map and review the above information with students. Explain that they will be creating a collage of an elephant that is decorated for a festival in India. Demonstrate the steps as students follow along.

Materials

- photographs of elephants
- 9- by 9-inch white drawing paper
- pencils
- crayons or colored pencils
- scissors
- 9- by 9-inch colored paper
- glue
- sequins or glitter
- 12- by 12-inch colored paper (different color than 9-inch paper)
- child-safe scissors with a fancy edge
- 1- by 12-inch strips of colored paper
- pencils

Resources

For Teachers

Indian Art by Vidya Dehejia (Phaidon Press, 1997). Written by the curator of the Smithsonian's Indian and Southeast Asian art collections, this book covers thousands of years of art in India.

Virginia Museum of Fine Art
http://www.vmfa.state.va.us/worlds/worlds_intro.html Based on an exhibition, this site provides an in-depth look at Indian painting.

For Students

Elephant Dance: Memories of India by Theresa Heine (Barefoot Books, 2004). In this picture book featuring colorful, folk-style illustrations, Ravi's grandfather describes life in his homeland of India.

Elephant Prince: The Story of Ganesh by Amy Novesky (Mandala, 2004). An authentic retelling of the Hindu myth explaining how the god Ganesh came to acquire his elephant head.

Directions

1 Have students use photos for reference as they draw on white paper an outline of an elephant from side view.

2 Draw a patterned blanket on the elephant's back. Draw jewelry on the head and feet of the elephant.

3 Use crayons or colored pencils to color the elephant. Press heavily to achieve dense colors.

4 Cut out the elephant and glue it to the center of the 9- by 9-inch paper. Glue on sequins or glitter for decoration.

5 Glue the 9- by 9-inch paper to the center of the 12- by 12-inch paper.

6 Use the decorative scissors to cut a fancy edge on four 1- by 12-inch strips. Glue these strips around the 9-inch paper to create a border.

More Ideas

❖ Have students research animals that are or were considered important to different cultures, such as the cat in ancient Egypt.

New Year's Dragons

Students create a large, colorful dragon in this collaborative project that ties in to Chinese New Year.

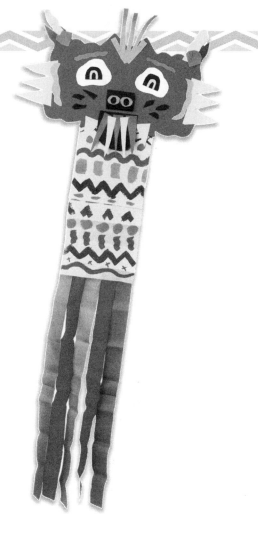

The folklore of many cultures includes mythical dragons. Most legends around the world characterize the dragon as a ferocious, fire-breathing beast that is feared by all. In Chinese stories and culture, the dragon is seen as a kind and friendly symbol of good luck and wealth. Since ancient times in China, the dragon has been the most important symbol of power. It is common to see the dragon motif on ancient art as well as in contemporary textiles, ceramics, and paintings. The dragon is also the fifth animal in the traditional 12-year animal zodiac.

The dragon is a popular feature in parades held during the Chinese New Year and other festivals. Large, colorful cloth dragons are carried by several dozen people who wind their way through the streets. As the dancers bring the dragon to life, they hope to prevent evil spirits from spoiling the new year. It is thought that good luck comes to all who see the dragon, and that the dragon's power can bring rainfall needed for each year's crops.

Getting Started

Place newspaper on tables and prepare the work space for painting. Have students wear smocks when painting.

Point out China on a map and review the above information with students. Show them photographs of mythical dragons and dragons created for Chinese New Year parades. Note the characteristics of the creatures: long body, tail, large eyes, fire-breathing nostrils, mouth, ears, horns, and claws. Divide the class into groups of three, and explain that each group will create its own large dragon. Demonstrate the steps as students follow along. (If desired, have students create their own projects. Set aside periods of time over several days to complete different sections of the project.)

Materials

- photographs of dragons from Chinese New Year parades
- 9- by 12-inch white or yellow paper (3 per group)
- newsprint
- red, yellow, blue, green, orange, and violet tempera paint
- paintbrushes
- water containers
- 12- by 18-inch colored construction paper
- pencils
- scissors
- construction paper scraps
- glue
- crepe paper streamers (or tissue paper sheets cut into long strips)

Resources

For Teachers

China: A New History by John King Fairbank and Merle Goldman (Belknap Press, 1998). A comprehensive look at China's history and culture.

For Students

The Dancing Dragon by Marcia K. Vaughan (Mondo, 1996). A Chinese-American girl and her family prepare for the Chinese New Year. The story concludes with a foldout dragon that can be displayed after reading.

The Last Dragon by Susan Miho Nunes (Clarion Books, 1997). A young Chinese-American boy is determined to restore a worn dragon costume.

Lion Dancer: Ernie Wan's Chinese New Year by Kate Waters (Scholastic, 1991). Ernie Wan describes his family's lunar New Year celebration. Includes color photographs and a chart of the Chinese zodiac.

Directions

1 Give each group three sheets of 9- by 12-inch paper, one per student, and a set of paints. Have students write their names on the backs of their papers.

2 Explain to students that they will be creating the body of the dragon. Invite students to paint a design across their paper widthwise. When students have filled their pages with colorful designs, set the pages aside to dry.

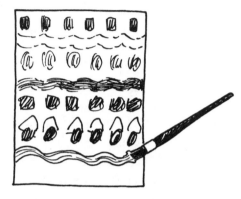

3 Demonstrate how to create the head. Fold a sheet of colored 12- by 18-inch construction paper in half widthwise. Draw the outline of half of the dragon's head around the edges of the paper. Cut out the head and unfold. Have each group work together to design and create a head for their dragon.

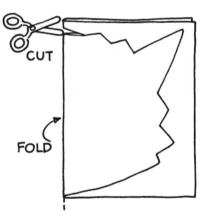

4 Show students how to glue construction paper scraps onto the head to add facial features and decorations. Encourage them to make some parts three-dimensional by curling and fanfolding the paper. Allow the glue to dry.

5 Once the body sheets have dried, show students how to glue or tape the 9-inch sides of the three pages together to create one long strip. Overlap the pages by about an inch. Let the glue dry.

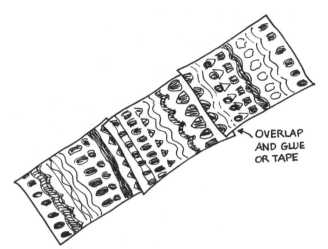

OVERLAP AND GLUE OR TAPE

6 Fanfold the paper, making each fold about two inches wide.

FOLD FORWARD   FOLD BACK

FOLD 2" PANES →

7 Glue the head to one end of the body. Add crepe paper streamers for the tail of the dragon. If crepe paper and tissue paper are unavailable, use strips of construction paper that have been fanfolded or curled instead.

More Ideas

Hold your own dragon parade! Let students carry their dragons down the hallways at a designated time for other classes to enjoy. Then display the dragons in the hallway along with pictures of Chinese New Year festivals and dragon parades. To create a dazzling display, use black paper to cover the bulletin board. Then use white crayon to draw fireworks and add glue and glitter over the lines. Attach the dragons to complete the festive display!

Flower Paintings

Students paint flowers in a style inspired by traditional Japanese ink painting.

Sumi-e is the Japanese word for black ink painting. This form of painting derived from Chinese calligraphy, which has been practiced for thousands of years in Asia. Although Sumi-e is simplistic in style, it is a challenging artistic form that is marked by spontaneity and flow. Artists aim to capture the true essence or life spirit of the subject being painted, rather than depict a realistic representation of it.

The quality of the brushstroke is an important aspect of this style of painting. Although only black ink is used in traditional sumi-e, the painter achieves a range of tones by the way the paint is applied. Factors such as the amount of ink on the brush, the amount of pressure applied, the speed of the stroke, and the angle at which the brush is held all contribute to the overall effect. The painter also makes use of the white paper in the composition. Traditional subject matter includes plants, flowers, trees, and landscapes.

Getting Started

When choosing the flowers or branch for the subject matter, look for something that will lend itself to an interesting composition, such as long stems or leaves. Arrange the flower or branch so that a large portion of it extends from the container or vase.

Place newspaper on tables and prepare the work space for painting. Have students wear smocks for this project.

Point out Japan on a map and review the above information with students. Show them several photographs of Japanese ink paintings and note characteristics such as line quality, subject matter, composition, and range of shades. Then demonstrate the steps as students follow along.

Materials

- photographs of Japanese ink paintings
- fresh flowers (or a branch with leaves) in a container or vase
- newsprint
- 12- by 18-inch heavy white drawing paper or watercolor paper
- black watercolor paint
- medium watercolor brushes
- water containers

Directions

1. Before beginning the project, provide newsprint and invite students to practice using black watercolor paint. Encourage them to experiment with the paint in different ways, such as using paint that has been mixed with more or less water, applying more or less paint to the brush, using the tip of the brush and the side of the brush, pulling the brush quickly or slowly across the page, and moving the brush in straight or curved lines.

2. Display the flowers where students can easily observe them. Ask students to describe what they see and what feelings the flowers evoke. (Although many sumi-e painters paint from memory, most students will benefit from observing the subject matter.) Tell students that they will paint the flowers using only black paint and any shades of gray they can create by varying the use of water and paint.

3. Position the paper either horizontally or vertically, depending upon the type of flower and the composition you would like to create. Imagine how the composition will look on the page. You might choose only one section of the flower to paint. (Try not to include the container or vase in the painting.)

4. It might be helpful to first paint the larger areas or lines using bold strokes. Encourage students to use the whole paper for their composition. Discuss the different kinds of brushstrokes they experimented with and encourage them to try different kinds as they are painting. Remind them not to layer the paint so that brushstrokes look fresh.

5. Add details to your painting. Let dry.

More Ideas

Have students use their paintings as subjects for haiku poems. Display the poems and paintings together.

Resources

For Teachers

Japanese Ink Painting: The Art of Sumi-e by Naomi Okamoto (Sterling, 1996). This helpful guide also explores the philosophy behind sumi-e.

Japanese Ink Painting: Beginner's Guide to Sumi-E by Susan Frame (Sterling, 2002). A step-by-step guide to creating Japanese ink pictures.

These Web sites provide examples of Japanese ink paintings.

Smithsonian: Freer and Sackler Galleries
http://www.asia.si.edu

Tokyo National Museum
http://www.tnm.jp/en/servlet/Con?pageId=X00&processId=00

The Virtual Museum of Japanese Arts
http://web-japan.org/museum/menu.html

For Students

I Live in Tokyo by Mari Takabayashi (Houghton Mifflin, 2001). In this colorful picture book, a young girl in Tokyo shares monthly traditions throughout a calendar year.

Tea With Milk by Allen Say (Houghton Mifflin, 1999). In this moving story, a young Japanese woman living in California moves back to Japan with her family and struggles to adapt to her new life there.

Aboriginal Bark Paintings

Students depict animals in a style inspired by the bark paintings of the Aborigines in Arnhem Land.

Australian Aborigines are the modern descendants of the first people to live in Australia. Archaeologists believe that the Aborigines may have inhabited Australia and its islands for more than 60,000 years. Many Aboriginal artists continue to paint in the traditional styles of their ancestors. Through their paintings, Aboriginal artists connect to the past and keep an important part of their culture alive.

The process of bark painting begins by removing a large strip of bark from a eucalyptus tree. The bark is flattened, scraped, and smoothed. Once the bark has dried, it is painted. The traditional colors of paint are red, black, white, and yellow and are applied with brushes made from grass, stems, twigs, feathers, or other materials. The subject matter often includes people, landforms, plants, animals, or myths. Artists often use an X-ray style of painting that shows the internal organs and skeletons of animals. Typical decorative patterns include fine lines, dots, crosshatching, and circles.

Getting Started

Point out Australia on a map and review the above information with students. Explain that they will create a project in the style of the bark paintings from the Aborigines in Arnhem Land, which is in Australia's Northern Territory. Next, show photographs of Aboriginal bark paintings and the animals typically depicted in them (such as kangaroos, emus, crocodiles, snakes, and fish), and discuss the X-ray style that is used. Ask students to use their imagination and think about how they could paint an abstract design to depict the animal and its internal details, such as the skeleton, heart, and lungs. Demonstrate the steps as students follow along.

Materials

- photographs of Aboriginal bark paintings and of animals depicted in them
- 12- by 16-inch brown craft paper or brown paper bags (cut to size)
- brown, red, and yellow tempera paint
- large, wide paintbrushes
- water containers
- colored pencils (browns, reds, yellows, white, and black)

Directions

1 Tear the edges of the craft paper or brown paper bags to form a rough edge.

2 Position the paper horizontally. Mix together brown and red paint for the background. To create a lighter color, add a bit of yellow paint. Use a large brush and a small amount of paint to paint the background. Paint in large strokes horizontally across the page to represent the texture of the bark. (This step is optional. If desired, paint or draw the animal directly on the brown paper using paint, colored pencils, or markers.) While the paper is drying, sketch several ideas for your painting. If the paper curls up after it has dried, place books on top of it to flatten it.

3 Using a light-colored pencil, draw the outline of your animal so that it fills the paper, keeping the shapes large. Refer to a photograph of the animal as needed. Use the entire paper for your composition.

4 Think about how you could abstractly represent the animal's skeleton or internal organs. This could be done with a design or pattern. Draw designs to represent the skeleton and internal organs.

5 Add more patterns to fill in the shapes within the figure. Try colorful dots, lines, crosshatching, and so on. Fill as much of the animal as possible.

More Ideas

Have students study other kinds of Aboriginal art, such as dream paintings, rock paintings, and carved emu eggs. Introduce them to the didgeridoo, a traditional Aboriginal instrument, and play a CD or audiocassette featuring this instrument.

Resources

For Teachers

Aboriginal Art of Australia: Exploring Cultural Traditions by Carol Finley (Lerner, 1999). Written for older students, this book explores Aboriginal art from several Australian regions.

Dreamings: The Art of Aboriginal Australia by Peter Sutton (George Braziller, 1997). This beautiful volume from the South Australia Museum and the Asia Society Galleries examines Aboriginal art and its connection to Dreamtime.

Museum Victoria
http://www.museum.
vic.gov.au/collections/
indigenous/collections.asp

For Students

Animal Dreaming: An Aboriginal Dreamtime Story by Paul Morin (Silver Whistle Books, 1998). An Aboriginal elder shares a creation story with a young boy.

Ernie Dances to the Didgeridoo by Alison Lester (Houghton Mifflin, 2001). In this picture book, Ernie spends a year in Arnhem Land and sends his friends letters about his experiences there.

Going for Oysters by Jeanie Adams (Albert Whitman, 1993). This book tells the story of an Aboriginal family coming together for a weekend of camping, gathering oysters, cooking, and other activities.

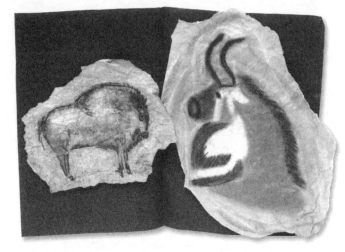

Lascaux Cave Drawings

Students use chalk or pastels to create Stone Age cave art.

Cave paintings and engravings provide valuable clues to the culture and beliefs of people from prehistoric times. In 1940 four teenagers accidentally discovered the Lascaux (lahs-KOH) Cave in southern France. Its walls contain rich, colorful paintings that are 15,000 to 17,000 years old and show lifelike images of man and animals such as bulls, horses, bison, deer, and even a rhinoceros. The cave also shows handprints and abstract patterns and markings, such as circles, dots, and zigzags. Natural clay was used to create yellow and red colors, while black was made from the carbon of burnt wood. Artists painted the limestone cave walls with brushes made from animal hair or crushed twigs. Some historians consider these detailed works the finest art ever found from the Paleolithic era (early Stone Age). France closed the cave to the public in 1963 due to deterioration of the paintings. Today only a replica is open to the public.

Getting Started

Have students wear smocks for this project. Point out France on a map and review the above information with students. Show them several photographs of Lascaux cave paintings and note the animals depicted, the colors, and the lively style of the art. Then demonstrate the steps as students follow along. Encourage them to use the photographs of the cave paintings for reference as they complete their project.

Materials

- pictures of prehistoric animals and photographs of Lascaux cave paintings
- brown craft paper or paper bags (cut open)
- black crayons
- yellow, brown, white, and red chalk or pastels
- paper towels or tissues
- glue
- newspaper
- 9- by 12- or 12- by 18-inch black paper

Directions

1 Tear a piece of brown paper to the size you would like for your animal drawing. Plan to fit two animal drawings on a sheet of 9- by 12-inch or 12- by 18-inch paper.

2 Use a black crayon to lightly sketch the outline of the animal (either the entire animal or its head).

3 Invite students to imagine that the sun is shining on their animal. Use white and yellow chalk or pastels to show the sunlight on part of the animal's back or head. Color the rest of the animal with red and brown chalk or pastels, using darker colors on the underside of the animal.

4 Blend the colors together using a paper towel or tissue wrapped around your finger.

5 Gently crumble the entire picture and then pull the edges to smooth it out. The results will produce a rough texture similar to that of a cave wall.

6 Draw a second animal on a separate piece of brown paper.

Resources

For Teachers

The Cave of Lascaux
http://www.culture.fr/
culture/arcnat/lascaux/en
The official site of the
Lascaux Cave includes useful
information and photos.

The Cave of Lascaux by Mario
Ruspoli (Harry N. Abrams,
1987). A journey into
France's famous prehistoric
cave, which is now closed
to the public. Includes
photographs, scientific
data, and text that details
the photographic project.

Painters of the Caves by
Patricia Lauber (National
Geographic, 1998). This
book for older students is
worth including in a lower
grade classroom reference
collection. Sections can be
read aloud or paraphrased.

7 Place the two animals close together on a sheet of black paper. Before gluing the animals onto the black paper, crumble small scraps of newspaper and place these under the animals. Then glue the animals onto the black paper. The stuffing behind the animals will create an uneven surface to represent a cave wall.

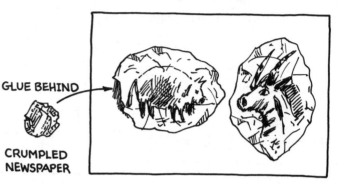

GLUE BEHIND

CRUMPLED NEWSPAPER

More Ideas

⬧ Display students' projects close together to create a story. Invite students to write about what the pictures might represent.

⬧ After researching the Stone Age, have students write a journal describing the routines in a day in the life of a person who lived during this time.

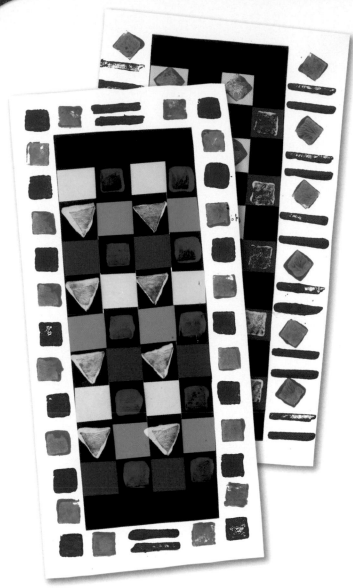

GHANA
**Woven Paper
Kente Cloth**
page 7

BURKINA FASO
Painted Masks
page 10

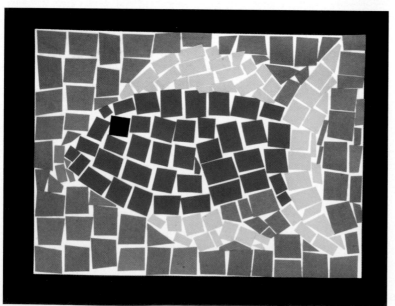

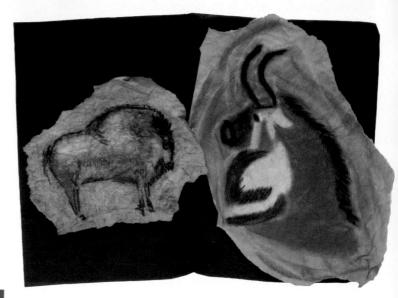

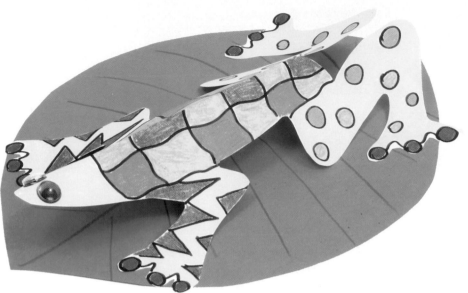

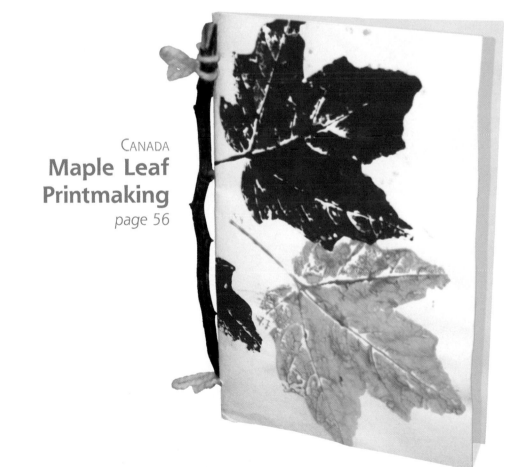

Delft Windmill Paintings

Students paint windmills in the tradition of delftware ceramic tiles from the Netherlands.

Delft or delftware is blue and white tin-glazed pottery that originated in the Netherlands in the 1600s around the town of Delft. Original delft often portrayed designs with bird or flower motifs inspired by designs from China. Dutch artists later incorporated traditional Dutch images and landscapes, including people, windmills, farmhouses, boats, animals, flowers, and birds. The designs are shown in tints of blue on white surfaces, and are found on tiles, tableware, ornaments, and ceramic wooden shoes. Delftware is world renowned, as are Holland's windmills. Windmills have graced Holland's countryside for centuries. They appear in a variety of shapes and sizes and have practical applications such as milling grain, pumping water, threshing, and sawing.

Getting Started

Place newspaper on tables and prepare the work space for painting. Have students wear smocks for this project.

Point out the Netherlands on a map and review the above information with students. Show them several photographs of windmills and examples of delftware. Then demonstrate the steps as students follow along.

Materials

- photographs of windmills and delftware
- 8- by 8-inch heavy white paper
- pencils
- blue and white tempera paint
- paper plates
- craft sticks
- small paintbrushes
- water containers
- glue
- 9- by 9-inch blue construction paper

Resources

For Teachers

Rijksmuseum
http://www.rijksmuseum.
nl/collectie/ontdekde
collectie?lang=en

Use the search engine
to locate examples of
delftware in the online
collection.

For Students

Katjie the Windmill Cat by
Gretchen Woelfle
(Candlewick, 2001). This
delightful picture book is
based on the true historical
story of a cat that saves
a baby in a flood. The
illustrations include
delft tiles.

Directions

1 In pencil, lightly
draw a tulip in each
of the four corners
of the white paper.
Then lightly draw a
windmill in the
center of the page.

2 Around the windmill,
lightly draw a land-
scape that includes
swirling clouds,
grass, water, a fence,
a boat, or a tree.
Add details to the
windmill, such as
windows, doors,
and patterns on
the blades. Keep
the drawing simple.

3 Place a small amount of blue and white paint on the paper
plate. Use a craft stick to mix together different amounts
of blue and white paint to create various tints of blue. It is
important to keep some of the original paint colors, as well
as to mix new shades. Do not stir all the paint together.

4 Use a paintbrush to paint over the sketch. Let dry. Add
details to complete the painting. Create contrast by painting
dark colors on top of light, or light next to dark.

5 Glue the painting to the center of the blue paper.

More Ideas

Students may be familiar with modern windmills. In many areas
they are now being used to generate electricity and are built of
metal. Compare and contrast the original Dutch windmills with
modern windmills.

Cut-Paper Viking Ships

Students make a Viking ship with a cut-paper collage and watercolor paints.

The Vikings were Scandinavians who raided coastal and riverside towns of Europe and the British Isles from the 9th century to 11th century. They were excellent shipbuilders and sailors. Their ships were constructed of wood and varied in size, depending on whether the ship was to be used for trade or battle.

Viking trading ships, or *knorrs*, were about 50 feet long. Warships, or longships, ranged in length from 65 to 95 feet. Viking warships sailed well in rough seas or calm waters. They were equipped with square or rectangular sails and many sets of oars. The front end of the ship curved gracefully upward and sometimes ended with a carved dragonhead. The dragon symbolized power and was thought to protect the ship and its crew from evil spirits. Many vessels were elaborately carved or decorated with painted shields.

Getting Started

Place newspaper on tables and prepare the work space for painting. Have students wear smocks for this project. Point out Norway on a map and review the above information with students. Show them photographs of Viking ships. Then demonstrate the steps as students follow along.

Materials

- photographs of Viking ships
- 9- by 12-inch white drawing paper
- watercolor paints
- watercolor brushes
- water containers
- 12- by 12-inch plastic wrap (one sheet per child)
- 12- by 18-inch blue or white construction paper
- glue
- crayons
- 9- by 12-inch brown construction paper
- pencils
- scissors
- black markers or crayons
- 9- by 12-inch white construction paper

Directions

1 Position the 9- by 12-inch white paper horizontally. Dip a paintbrush in clean water and gently brush over the paper to wet it. Select paint colors to represent the water: blues, greens, and small amounts of purple. While the paper is wet, lightly paint wavy lines. Let the colors of the paint blend and run into one another. Paint quickly so that the colors do not become muddied. Do not scrub the paper with the brush while the paint is wet.

2 To create texture that resembles water, crumple the plastic wrap and place it on top of the wet painting. Gently press it on top of the paper (some of the wrap will not be touching the painting). Lay flat to dry.

3 Gently peel the plastic wrap off the painting. To make waves, position the paper vertically and tear sections of the painting into wavy lines. Use one hand to hold the paper and the other to tear.

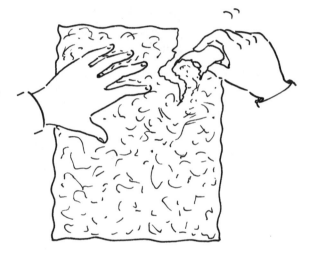

4 Position the 12- by 18-inch paper vertically. Glue the waves to the page, starting at the bottom and working your way up about a third of the page. Overlap the waves to make them look more realistic and also to provide a space into which you can tuck the ship.

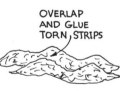

OVERLAP AND GLUE TORN STRIPS

5 To complete the sky, use crayons to add clouds, a sunset, or a stormy sky.

6 Position the brown paper horizontally. Using a pencil, draw the ship as large as possible and add a dragon head if desired. Refer to the photographs for reference. Cut out the ship.

7 Use a black marker or crayon to draw shields and designs on the ship.

8 Tuck the boat under a wave so that the bottom of the boat is covered a bit. Glue the boat in place.

9 Cut sails from the white construction paper. Use crayons to draw stripes and designs on the sails. Glue them in place.

More Ideas

❖ Have students trace the Vikings' voyages on a world map.

❖ Invite students to research and write a piece of historical fiction about what it would be like to travel on the ship they created. Post the stories beside the ships for a Viking display.

Resources

For Teachers

BBC School Links: The Vikings
http://www.bbc.co.uk/schools/vikings/index.shtml
Information about Vikings, with additional useful Web links.

Smithsonian Museum of Natural History Vikings: The North Atlantic Saga
http://www.mnh.si.edu/vikings
This information-packed site includes an online exhibit, teacher's guide, maps, Web links, and more.

For Students

The Vikings (Spotlights) by Neil Grant (Oxford University Press, 1998). Written for older students, this resource introduces artifacts, tools, and other aspects of Vikings' daily lives.

The Real Vikings by Gilda Berger (National Geographic, 2003). While written for slightly older students, this informative account of Viking history can serve as a visual reference for younger students.

Pysanky Egg Paintings

Students use watercolor and glue to create a Ukrainian egg design.

Pysanky, the art of the decorated egg, is an ancient and beautiful form of folk art from the Ukraine. These small works of art are for ornamental use and are widely admired and collected. Pysanky are traditionally created and exchanged among Ukrainian family members and friends in springtime and at Easter. The traditions behind the designs are as varied as the designs themselves. Designs include geometric shapes, hearts, bands, religious symbols, flowers, animals, birds, and agricultural components.

Pysanky are made using a wax-resist method. The process involves applying hot beeswax to a white egg with a writing tool called a *kistka*. When the wax drawing is complete, the egg is dipped in a light-colored dye, such as yellow, and then dried. A second design is drawn in wax upon the first color. When complete, the egg is dipped into a darker dye. The process continues, alternating between drawing and dying. When a pysanka (the singular term for one egg) is finished, the wax is removed and the egg is coated with shellac or varnish.

Getting Started

In advance, prepare black glue by mixing one part black tempera paint and five parts white glue. Mix a large amount in a bowl or container and refill the glue bottles.

Materials

- black tempera paint
- white glue
- mixing bowl or container
- egg template (page 41)
- design sheet (page 42)
- *Rechenka's Eggs* by Patricia Polacco
- photographs or samples of decorated pysanky eggs
- 9- by 12-inch watercolor paper or heavy white drawing paper
- pencils
- watercolor paints
- watercolor brushes
- water containers
- scissors
- 10- by 12-inch black or colored construction paper

Make copies of the egg template and design sheet. Enlarge the egg template slightly to fit a 9- by 12-inch page. If you would like to create larger eggs on 12- by 18-inch paper, draw and copy a larger template for students to trace. Place newspaper on tables and prepare the work space for painting. Have students wear smocks for this project.

Read aloud *Rechenka's Eggs*, by Patricia Polacco (Philomel, 1988). Point out Ukraine on a map and review the information on page 38 with students. Show photographs or samples of decorated eggs. Then demonstrate the steps as students follow along.

Directions

1 Trace the egg template onto white paper. Use a pencil to divide the egg into quarters, or into even horizontal sections. You might curve the lines slightly.

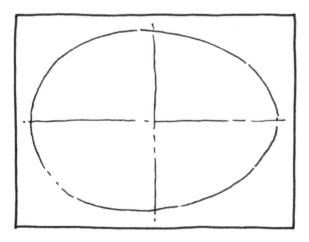

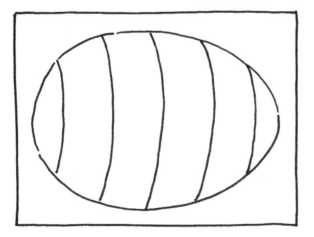

Resources

For Teachers

Decorating Eggs: Exquisite Designs With Wax and Dye by Jane Pollak (Sterling, 1996). Learn how to apply intricate designs onto eggshells using a wax-and-dye technique.

Eggs Beautiful: How to Make Ukrainian Easter Eggs by Johanna Luciow (Ukrainian Gift Shop, 1975). Learn how to create your own pysanky eggs with this step-by-step guide.

For Students

Rechenka's Eggs by Patricia Polacco (Philomel, 1988). An old woman who works all year to decorate eggs for the Easter festival takes in a wounded goose. When an accident destroys the woman's eggs, the goose saves the day with a series of colorful surprises!

Ukrainian Egg Decoration: A Holiday Tradition by Ann Stalcup (Powerkids Press, 1999). Includes a simple step-by-step egg project for children and explains how the tradition of decorating pysanky eggs evolved.

2 Discuss the traditional designs on the reproducible sheet. Refer to the sheet for ideas to decorate the egg. Draw decorations on your egg, following the Ukrainian style. Draw repeated designs in each section of the egg. It is important to keep the designs simple so that it will be easier to apply the glue later.

3 When the design is complete, cover all lines with a thin line of black glue. If the glue separates, reapply the glue so that it forms a continuous line. Lay flat to dry.

4 Use watercolor paints to paint the areas between the glue lines. The glue will act as a barrier and keep the color contained within the areas painted (similar to the wax used for painting real eggs). Create a pattern with the watercolors, using no more than four or five colors. Let dry.

5 Cut out the eggs and glue them on black or colored construction paper.

More Ideas

Display the completed eggs alongside a world map showing Ukraine. Add photographs of decorated eggs and an explanation of the process.

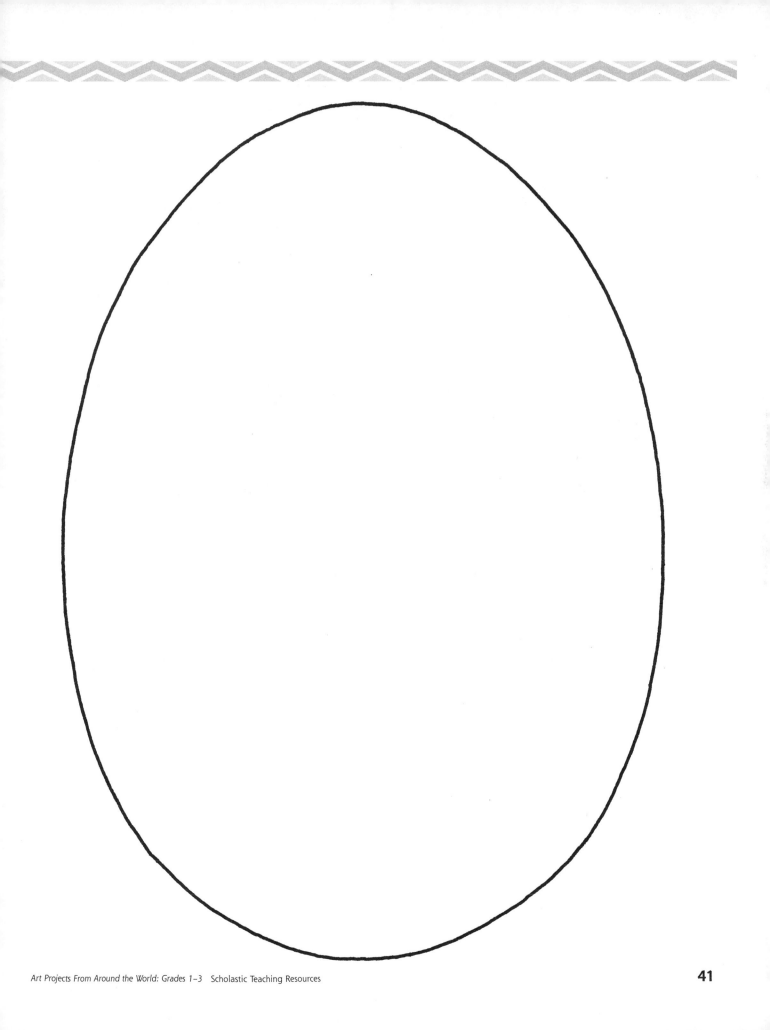

Traditional Pysanky Designs

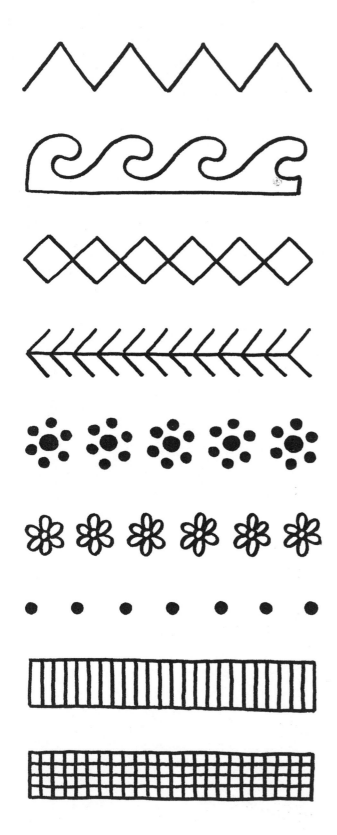

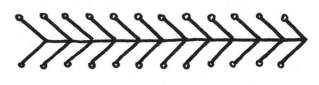
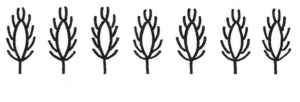

Tin Ornaments

Students make a decorative ornament with aluminum foil and markers.

Metalworking has been an art form in Mexico since pre-Columbian times. Tin is an inexpensive metal used by Mexican artisans to create beautiful decorative and religious objects as well as folk art. Tin has tremendous flexibility, which allows the metal to be pressed, hammered, punched, cut, etched, embossed, or painted. Frames, crosses, niches, boxes, sconces, mirrors, luminaries, and ornaments are some of the items made by Mexican tinsmiths. These pieces can be rustic in color or painted. Ornaments are brightly painted and often portray celestial images such as stars and the sun, religious themes such as crosses and angels, or nature native to Mexico, including animals, fish, birds, and cactus plants.

Getting Started

Place the square of cardboard on top of the aluminum foil. Fold the edges and tape the back on the four sides. An adult should complete this step in advance so that students do not handle the sharp-edged, heavy-duty foil.

Point out Mexico on a map and review the above information with students. Show them photographs of tin ornaments and sun designs. Then demonstrate the steps as students follow along.

Materials

- photographs of tin ornaments and sun designs
- 8-inch square of heavy-duty aluminum foil
- 5-inch cardboard square
- tape
- pencils (sharp and dull)
- 5-inch white drawing paper
- newspaper
- permanent markers (use only in a well-ventilated area)
- 6-inch squares of colored paper
- 7-inch squares of colored paper (different color than 6-inch squares)
- hole punch (optional)
- ribbon or yarn (optional)

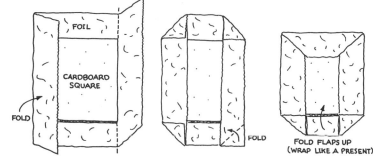

FOIL

CARDBOARD SQUARE

FOLD

FOLD

FOLD FLAPS UP
(WRAP LIKE A PRESENT)

TAPE BACK

Resources

For Teachers

The Crafts of Mexico by Margarita de Orellana and Alberto Ruy Sanchez (Smithsonian, 2004). Features color photos and information about different kinds of Mexican crafts, including tinwork, textiles, ceramics, and more.

Latin American Arts and Cultures by Dorothy Chaplik (Davis, 2001). This book for older students surveys Latin American art from pre-Columbian times to the present.

Mexican Art and Culture by Elizabeth Lewis (Raintree, 2005). Written for older students, this book provides an overview of the history of Mexican art.

Scholastic's Global Trek: Mexico
http://teacher.scholastic.com/activities/globaltrek/destinations/mexico.htm
Features information about Mexico's history and culture. Appropriate for older students.

Smithsonian National Museum of the American Indian
Great Masters of Mexican Folk Art
http://www.nmai.si.edu/exhibitions/gm/html_eng.html
This Web site includes information about different kinds of Mexican folk art, including works in metal, paper, and clay.

For Students

Let's Go Traveling in Mexico by Robin Rector Krupp (HarperCollins, 1996). A mythical creature gives a lively tour of sites throughout Mexico and provides engaging information about the country's culture, history, and geography.

My Mexico/México Mío by Tony Johnston (Putnam, 1999). Poems in English and Spanish impart a sense of life in Mexico.

Directions

1 Draw a sun design on the white paper.

2 Place the white paper on top of the foil-wrapped cardboard square. Fold newspaper into a square and place it in between the white paper and the foil. Use a dull pencil to go over the lines on the white paper. The newspaper will act as a cushion so that the pencil does not tear the foil.

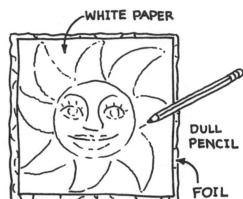

WHITE PAPER
DULL PENCIL
FOIL

3 Use permanent markers to color the ornament. Add line designs such as swirls, dots, and zigzags.

4 Glue the foil and cardboard sun to the center of a 6-inch colored square of paper. Then glue the 6-inch paper to the center of a 7-inch square of paper.

More Ideas

❖ To hang the ornament, use a hole punch to punch a small hole at the top. (An adult should complete this step.) Tie a ribbon or a piece of yarn through the hole.

❖ Make tin ornaments using other traditional designs from Mexico, such as birds, fish, and other animals.

Caribbean Houses

Students create a colorful Caribbean-style house using paint, markers, and cut paper.

The architecture of Caribbean homes is strongly influenced by the tropical climate. Caribbean-style houses, called case houses, are found throughout the Caribbean Islands. These homes are designed with an open-air floor plan and are built with verandas, porches, and large doors and windows to take advantage of the gentle cooling breeze from the trade winds. Shutters help to keep the hot sun out of the dwelling, and also provide a quick way to close up the house when a hurricane approaches. Many Caribbean homes are painted pastel colors or sun-drenched hues to reflect their tropical surroundings. Architectural elements such as gingerbread fretwork, elaborate latticework, and grillwork are often used to enhance the festive flavor of these tropical homes.

Getting Started

Place newspaper on tables and prepare the work space for painting. Have students wear smocks for this project.

Point out the islands of the Caribbean on a map and review the above information with students. Show them photographs of Caribbean-style houses and encourage them to use these for reference as they complete their projects. You might play Reggae music while students are working. Then demonstrate the steps as students follow along.

Materials

- photographs of Caribbean-style houses from travel brochures or magazines
- 12- by 15-inch tagboard or heavy drawing paper
- pencils
- tempera paint in bright colors
- paintbrushes
- water containers
- markers (regular and fine point)
- colored pencils
- ruler
- scissors
- 1-inch cardboard squares (several for each student)
- glue
- 12- by 18-inch light blue, blue, turquoise, and purple construction paper
- 9- by 12-inch colored construction paper (green, brown, and other colors)
- 16- by 22-inch black paper (optional, for mounting)

Directions

1 Position the tagboard or heavy drawing paper horizontally. Using a pencil, draw a Caribbean-style house. Include features such as windows with shutters, a front porch, steps, and rock foundations.

Discuss details such as decorative woodwork and railings, but do not draw them at this time. This makes it easier to paint the base color of the house.

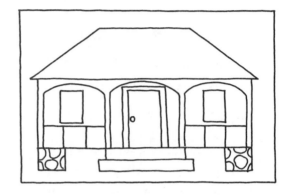

2 Use several bright colors to paint the roof, house, and porch. Let dry.

3 Use markers to draw details such as the porch railings, windowpanes, and rooflines (use a ruler as needed). If desired, draw fancy woodwork at the top of the porch.

4 Cut out the house. Glue together pairs of cardboard squares. Glue several of these to the back of the house. Glue the raised house to the light blue or turquoise background paper.

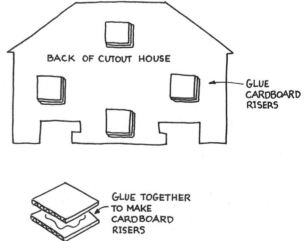

BACK OF CUTOUT HOUSE

GLUE CARDBOARD RISERS

GLUE TOGETHER TO MAKE CARDBOARD RISERS

5 Use cut paper to create ferns, palm trees, and flowering plants. Glue these around the outside of the house.

6 To create shutters, cut out rectangles from colored construction paper. Fold one edge of each rectangle. Use a fine-point marker or colored pencil to add lines to the shutters. Glue the folded edge onto a window.

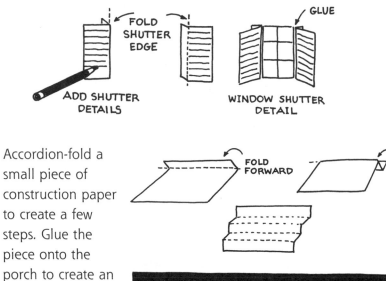

7 Accordion-fold a small piece of construction paper to create a few steps. Glue the piece onto the porch to create an inviting entrance to the house.

Resources

For Teachers

A Brief History of the Caribbean by Jan Rogonzinski (Plume, 1994). Examines the Caribbean's rich history.

Caribbean Style by Suzanne Slesin et al. (Three Rivers Press, 1998). More than 600 color photos guide readers through representative Caribbean architecture.

For Students

Coconut Kind of Day: Island Poems by Lynn Joseph (Puffin, 1992). In this beautifully illustrated book, 13 poems take readers through a day with a Caribbean family.

My Little Island by Frane Lessac (Harper, 1987). A young boy visits a Caribbean island in this celebration of island life.

More Ideas

◈ Invite students to write a poem about their "cool" Caribbean house.

◈ Have students choose a Caribbean island and research it. Then invite them to present their findings to the class. Make an enlarged map of the Caribbean and have students color their island.

Rain Sticks

Students use recyclable materials to create a musical instrument.

The Atacama Desert in northern Chile is one of the world's driest regions. In certain sections rainfall does not register at all. The Diaguita people from this region make and use rain sticks. Used in Diaguita ceremonies, these rain sticks are thought to bring needed rain to the arid countryside. Rain sticks are created from the dead stalks of cactus plants. Spines or thorns from the plant are driven through dead stalk in a spiral formation. Small pebbles are placed inside, and the ends are capped. When inverted, the pebbles trickle down inside the stalk, hit the thorns as they fall, and create a soothing, rainlike sound. Rain sticks vary in straightness, diameter, and texture. They are often decorated with colorful yarn bands or painted. These instruments have been adopted by musicians around the world and in recent years have become popular folk art pieces.

Getting Started

Point out Chile on a map and review the above information with students. Show them photographs of rain sticks, or if possible bring in a rain stick. Then demonstrate the steps as students follow along.

Directions

1 Twist aluminum foil into a snakelike form as long as the paper tube. Wrap the foil "snake" around the dowel and place it inside the tube.

WRAP FOIL AROUND DOWEL

Materials

- photographs or samples of rain sticks
- empty wrapping paper tube (no longer than 2 feet)
- aluminum foil
- wooden dowel, cut to length of tube
- scissors
- 5-inch paper circles (2 per student)
- masking tape
- dried beans, rice, or unpopped popcorn kernels
- 5-inch circles of burlap (2 per student)
- glue
- rubber bands (2 per student)
- markers
- yarn or string
- beads

2 Cover one end of the tube with paper and masking tape.

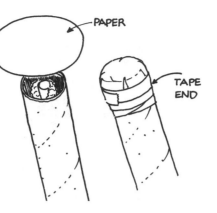

PAPER

TAPE END

3 Place one-half cup or more of beans, rice, or unpopped corn kernels in the tube. Cover the open end with paper and tape to secure. Listen to see if beans fall too fast. If they do, open the tube and wrap more foil around the dowel.

4 Place the burlap circles over the ends of the tube and glue the edges in place. Secure with rubber bands. (An adult should complete this step.)

SECURE WITH RUBBER BAND

5 Use markers to draw designs resembling the texture of a cactus plant on the tube. For added decoration, tie yarn around each end of the tube and attach beads to the ends of the yarn.

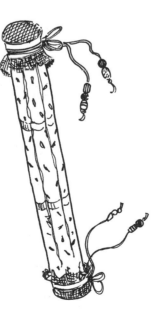

More Ideas

❖ Have students research why rain sticks were used in dry climates.

❖ Create a word bank of words to describe the rain sticks, such as *soothing, calming, natural, pleasant,* and *rhythmic.*

❖ Play some soothing nature music. Invite students to tilt their rain sticks to the rhythm.

Resources

For Teachers

The History of Chile by John L. Rector (Palgrave Macmillan, 2005). Examines Chile's social, cultural, and political development from its indigenous people to today's democracy.

For Students

Chile (New True Books) by Karen Jacobsen (Children's Press, 1991). A basic introduction to Chile's history, geography, and culture.

Mariana and the Merchild: A Folk Tale from Chile by Caroline Pitcher (William B. Eerdman, 2000). A lonely old woman is comforted by the arrival of a merchild in a seashell. The friends she makes as she raises the child comfort her when the child must return to the sea.

Rain Forest Puppets

Students create a puppet of a rain forest creature.

The Amazon Rain Forest, also known as Amazonia, covers much of northern South America. Approximately two-thirds of the rain forest is located in Brazil. It also occupies parts of Bolivia, Peru, Ecuador, Colombia, Venezuela, Guyana, Suriname, and French Guiana. This hot environment with abundant rainfall contains a wider variety of plant and animal life than any other place in the world.

The Amazon Rain Forest consists of four levels or communities: the emergent (the tallest treetops), the canopy (leafy treetops), the understory (between the leaves and the ground), and the forest floor. Each level has unique ecosystems, plants, and animals adapted to that system. Insects such as moths, butterflies, bees, and spiders are found at all levels. Deer, tapir, giant anteaters, hogs, rodents, scorpions, and other creatures make the floor their home. Chimps, jaguars, and ocelots live both on the floor and in the understory. Animals such as bats, monkeys, parrots, toucans, lizards, and snakes live in the canopy. Scientists believe that millions of species of animals in the Amazon remain undiscovered.

Getting Started

In advance, have students choose the kind of animal for their puppet so that you know what color mouthpiece to create. Prepare a puppet mouthpiece for each student. See directions on page 51.

Point out the Amazon Rain Forest on a map and review the above information with students. You may want to read aloud a book about the rain forest (see Resources, page 52) or play a CD or audiocassette of sounds of the rain forest. Show students photographs of animals that live in the Amazon. Encourage students to refer to a photograph of their animal as they create their puppet. Then demonstrate the steps as students follow along.

Materials

- photographs of the Amazon Rain Forest and its animals
- 9- by 12-inch construction paper (various colors)
- pencils
- scissors
- glue
- markers
- tissue paper (various colors)
- CD or audiocassette of rain forest sounds (optional)

Directions for Puppet Mouthpiece

1 Fold a sheet of colored construction paper in thirds lengthwise. Flip over the paper and fold it in half as shown.

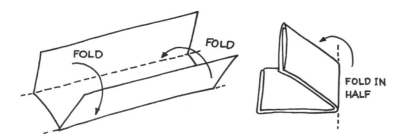

2 Fold the bottom edge back to meet the fold. Then fold the top edge back to meet the fold. Fold so that the open edges are on the outside. This will create pockets for fingers.

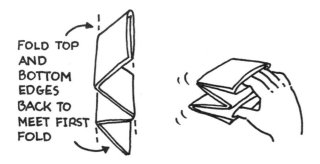

Directions for Puppet

1 Decide if your puppet will be vertical or horizontal, depending on the type of animal it is. Birds work well as vertical puppets and four-legged animals work well as horizontal puppets. (See photos of project samples.)

2 Choose a sheet of construction paper that is the body color of your animal. Sketch the body shape of the animal so that it fills the page. Cut out the shape. Students may need help with this step.

3 Add details to the animal's body by drawing or gluing on legs, claws, wings, spots, stripes, paper feathers, and so on. You might use tissue paper to create some of the animal's features.

Resources

For Teachers

PBS: Journey Into Amazonia
http://www.pbs.org/journey
intoamazonia
An information-packed site
about the geography, plants,
and animals of the Amazon
Rain Forest. Includes teacher
resources, Web links, and more.

For Students

*The Great Kapok Tree: A Tale of the
Amazon Rain Forest* by Lynne
Cherry (Gulliver, 1990). The
creatures of the rain forest save
a kapok tree from destruction.

Here Is the Tropical Rain Forest by
Madeleine Dunphy (Hyperion,
1997). An introduction to the
ecosystem of a rain forest.

*Nature's Green Umbrella: Tropical
Rain Forests* by Gail Gibbons
(Harper, 1997). Animals, plants,
and trees are clearly illustrated
and labeled in this informative
introduction to the rain forest.

4 Attach the mouthpiece to the body.

- If the puppet is horizontal, attach the body to the mouthpiece
  so that the body will rest on the puppeteer's arm. Then fold the
  sides down over the arm to give the puppet's body a three-
  dimensional appearance. (See jaguar in photo.)

- If the puppet is vertical, attach the
  body so that it hangs down from
  the mouthpiece in the puppeteer's
  hand. (See bird in photo.)

5 Add facial
features to the
mouthpiece by
gluing on cut
paper and
drawing details
with markers.
You might glue
a paper tongue
to the inside of
the mouthpiece.

More Ideas

- Have students research their animal. Invite them to use the
  information and work in groups to write a puppet play in which
  their puppets describe life in the Amazon Rain Forest.

- Create a bulletin board display that shows the different levels of
  a rain forest (the forest floor, the understory, the canopy, and the
  emergent layer). Display the animal puppets in the appropriate
  place, and add rain forest facts and labels.

Rain Forest Tree Frogs

Students make a pop-up tree frog with bright patterns.

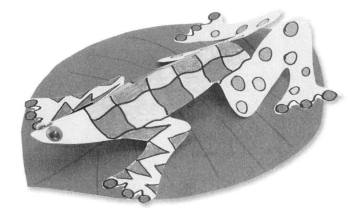

The Amazon Rain Forest, also known as Amazonia, covers much of northern South America. Approximately two-thirds of the rain forest is located in Brazil. It also occupies parts of Bolivia, Peru, Ecuador, Colombia, Venezuela, Guyana, Suriname, and French Guiana. The Amazon Rain Forest is home to a wide variety of tree frogs. Frogs are amphibians. They thrive in the rain forest climate, where the temperature is warm and rainfall is frequent. Tree frogs are adept climbers and spend most of their lives in bushes and trees. They have sticky pads on their toes that enable them to cling to moist vegetation. Most tree frogs range in length from less than one inch to about five inches. Many can change color to blend in with their surroundings. Some tree frogs, like the red-eyed tree frog, have a greenish coloring that serves as camouflage among leaves and vines. Others, like the poison dart frog, have colorful markings or spots in bright red, orange, green, yellow, and blue. These colors warn predators that they are poisonous.

Getting Started

In advance, make copies of the frog template. Point out the Amazon Rain Forest on a map and review the above information with students. This activity is an excellent companion to Rain Forest Puppets (pages 50–52). Show students photographs of tree frogs that live in the Amazon. Encourage students to use the photographs as inspiration for their project. Then demonstrate the steps as students follow along.

Materials

- photographs of different kinds of rain forest tree frogs
- frog template (page 55)
- 9- by 12-inch white paper
- scissors
- pencils
- black markers
- crayons, markers, or colored pencils
- wiggle eyes
- glue
- 9- by 12-inch green construction paper

Resources

For Teachers

Smithsonian National Zoological Park: Amazonia
http://nationalzoo.si.edu/Animals/Amazonia
This site about the park's Amazonia exhibit provides information about the Amazon Rain Forest and its wildlife.

For Students

Flashy, Fantastic Rain Forest Frogs by Dorothy Hinshaw (Walker, 1999). A close-up look at these rain forest creatures.

Poison Dart Frogs by Jennifer Owings Dewey (Boyds Mills Press, 1998). Describes the reasons poison dart frogs release their poison, other ways in which poison dart frogs defray predators, and how hunters obtain and use the poison for their own means.

Red-Eyed Tree Frog by Joy Cowley (Scholastic Press, 1999). Stunning color photographs and simple text narrate a day in the life of a tree frog living in the rain forest.

Directions

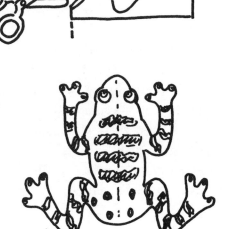

1 Fold the white paper in half lengthwise. Cut out the template and place it on the folded edge. Trace the template with a pencil. Cut out the shape.

2 Use a black marker to draw designs on the frog. The designs can be fanciful or realistic.

3 Color the patterns and designs with crayons, markers, or colored pencils.

4 Glue on two wiggle eyes.

5 Draw a large leaf shape on green paper. Cut out the shape. Draw veins with crayons or markers.

6 To make the frog pop up, press the crease on its back. Glue the frog's feet to the leaf so that the frog's body is sticking up a bit.

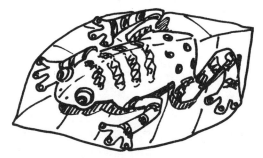

More Ideas

Create a display with a background of brown twine looped around to look like vines. Place the completed projects on top of the twine. To create an ecosystem, have students draw other animals that live in the rain forest.

Frog Template

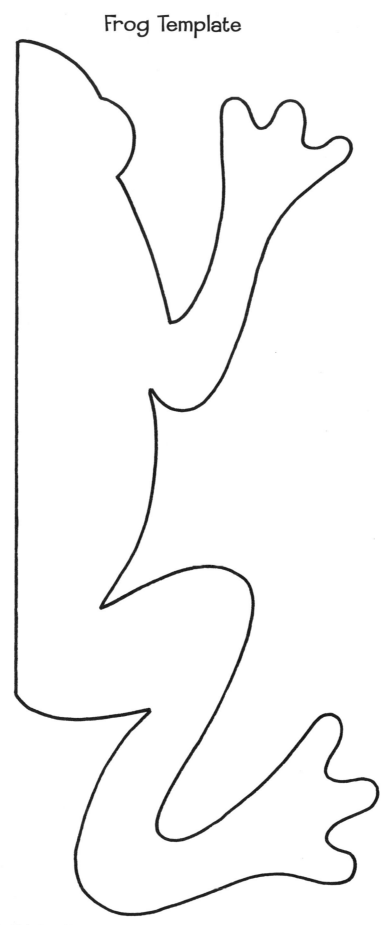

Maple Leaf Printmaking

Students experiment with printmaking to create a simple, autumn-themed book.

The maple leaf is the national symbol of Canada. It celebrates Canada's natural environment. The maple leaf began to serve as a symbol as early as 1700. It adorns Canadian coins and the national flag as well as the jersey of the Toronto Maple Leafs, a Canadian ice hockey team. The 11-pointed maple leaf on the flag is a sugar maple leaf. Sugar maples are native to Canada. They have brilliant autumnal foliage, with colors ranging from yellow to orange to fluorescent red-orange. Canadians produce delicious maple syrup and maple candy, made from the boiled sap of the sugar maple tree. Sugar maples are also an important source of hardwood timber. Sugar maple leaves are 3 to 5 inches long and equally wide, and most have five lobes.

Materials

- maple leaves and photographs of maple trees
- yellow and red tempera paint
- paper plates
- 9- by 12-inch white construction paper
- paintbrushes
- water containers
- paper towels
- hole punch
- 8½- by 11-inch white paper (3 sheets per student)
- 9-inch stick
- pencils
- 18-inch pieces of red, orange, or yellow yarn (1 per student)

Getting Started

Place newspaper on tables and prepare the work space for painting. Pour a small amount of paint onto the paper plates, one plate per color. Have students wear smocks for this project.

Point out Canada on a map and review the above information with students. Show students photographs of maple trees and have them examine the leaves. Then demonstrate the steps as students follow along.

Directions

1 Brush a thin layer of paint on the underside of the maple leaf, where the veins are raised.

2 Carefully place the leaf on the white construction paper, with the painted side facing down. Place a paper towel on top of the leaf and gently rub it to transfer the leaf print onto the paper.

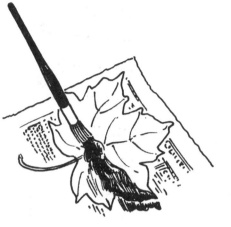

3 Remove the leaf and paint it a second time, using a different color. The colors will mix to create interesting new colors. Print the leaf in the same way. Continue painting and printing, allowing the leaves to overlap. Let dry.

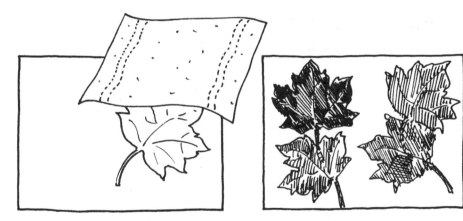

4 Fold the leaf-printed paper in half widthwise. Use a hole punch to make two holes one inch from the top and bottom of the page.

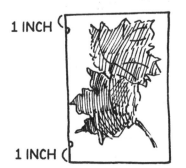

1 INCH

1 INCH

Resources

For Students

Canada (Rookie Read-About Geography) by David F. Marx (Children's Press, 2000). Color photos and easy-to-read text introduce students to Canada's history, culture, and geography.

The First Red Maple Leaf by Ludmilla Zeman (Tundra Books, 1997). In this original fable, a boy and his people find safety under a maple tree.

From Far and Wide: A Canadian Citizenship Scrapbook by Jo Bannatyne-Cugnet (Tundra Books, 2000). A young girl and her parents take part in a Canadian citizenship ceremony.

From Maple Trees to Maple Syrup by Krisin Thoennes Keller (First Facts Books, 2004). Photos, fun facts, and simple text describe the syrup-making process from tree to table.

The Sugaring-Off Party by Jonathan London (Dutton, 1995). In this warm story that takes place in Canada, Grandmother describes her first celebration of springtime sap.

TIP

If desired, cut two 5-inch pieces of yarn and tie them as bows around each end of the stick for decoration.

5 Fold three sheets of plain white paper in half widthwise. Place the folded pages inside the printed cover. Use a pencil to mark where to punch the holes on each page. Remove the pages and punch the holes.

6 Place the book pages inside the printed cover. Tie one end of the yarn around one end of the stick. Push the rest of the yarn through the hole and into the book. Pull the yarn through the other hole and tie it around the other end of the stick. Be sure to pull the yarn tightly to bind the book. (An adult should complete these steps or assist students.) If sticks are unavailable, the books can be bound with a piece of yarn tied through each hole.

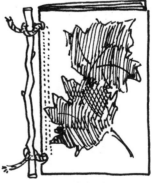

More Ideas

◆ Experiment with printmaking with vegetables or other objects.

◆ Make books using different printmaking materials.

Colonial Quilt Designs

Students work together to create a patriotic paper patchwork quilt.

Quilting was a traditional craft among young girls and women of the early American colonies. Quilts were fashioned of three layers of cloth and were hand-sewn with tiny stitches. Many quilts from the early 18th century were constructed of pieces of worn-out clothing or sewing scraps, since textiles from England were expensive and scarce. Patchwork quilts resemble mosaics, with bits of fabric carefully pieced together to form a pattern.

Quilting bees are social gatherings of small groups that work on one quilt at a time until each member has completed a quilt. Many traditional quilt designs, such as the log cabin, bear paw, wedding knot, and star of Bethlehem, have been passed down for generations and are still being used today.

Getting Started

Point out the United States on a map and review the above information with students. Show students photographs of quilts (or real quilts, if available) and note the designs. Discuss how the names fit the styles of the quilt designs. Have students note the shapes, colors, and patterns in the quilts. Then demonstrate the steps as students follow along.

Materials

- photographs of quilts
- 12- by 12-inch white paper
- 3-inch red and blue paper squares (about 12 per student)
- 3-inch wallpaper squares with red, white, and blue patterns (optional)
- scissors
- glue sticks
- fine-tipped markers (optional)

Resources

For Teachers

The American Quilt: A History of Cloth and Comfort 1750–1950 by Roderick Kiracofe (Clarkson, Potter, 2004). Learn how to "read" historic quilts, using their fabrics, dyes, and patterns, in this comprehensive reference book.

Quilts! Quilts! Quilts! The Complete Guide to Quiltmaking by Diana McClun (Quilt Digest, 1988). This complete guide offers something for quilt-makers at every level.

For Students

Eight Hands Round: A Patchwork Alphabet by Ann Whitford Paul (HarperTrophy, 1996). The author explores possible inspirations for pioneer quilt patterns.

The Quilt by Ann Jonas (Greenwillow, 1984). A young girl's quilt comes to life.

The Quiltmaker's Gift by Jeff Brumbeau (Scholastic, 2001). In this original fable, a king learns an important lesson when he tries to acquire a quilt.

Directions

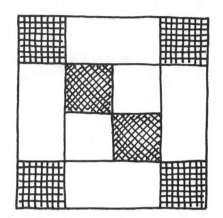

1. Choose eight colored squares and place them on the white background to create a pattern. (Use patterned wallpaper squares, if available, in addition to red and blue squares.) Remove some squares as needed to allow the white paper to be part of the design. Move the squares around the paper to create new patterns.

2. Cut some squares into triangles by folding two opposite corners together. Cut along the diagonal fold. Use these pieces to create a more complex pattern. Balance shapes and colors to create a pleasing design.

3. When you are satisfied with your quilt composition, lift the pieces one at a time and glue them onto the white background paper.

4. Display the finished quilt squares together to create one large class quilt.

More Ideas

- Have students use a fine-point marker to draw small lines to create the effect of stitching. They might draw straight lines that run in rows or more decorative designs.

- Have students sit in a circle to reenact a quilting bee.

Kachina Dolls

Inspired by the Hopi, students create a wooden sculpture.

In the Pueblo region, kachinas (ka-CHEE-nas) are believed to be the essential forms of objects or forces—animals, rain, sun, and death, to name a few. These forms or forces are thought to travel between the human world and the supernatural realm. Traditionally, each Pueblo society recognizes hundreds of distinct kachinas. These spirit beings are believed to visit Pueblo communities throughout the growing season, December to July, bringing renewal and good fortune to the land and its people. Wearing masks and costumes, Pueblo men perform ritual dances that blur the boundaries between the human and spirit worlds. Kachina dolls, called *tihu*, are figures carved of cottonwood roots made to represent the dancer.

The Hopi, a Pueblo people of northeastern Arizona, are well-known for their kachina dolls. Hopi dancers first make rough carvings of kachina dolls using large knives, and then refine their work with finer tools. Traditionally, the carved wood was coated with clay and then painted with natural dyes and pigments. Contemporary kachina makers frequently use commercial paints to finish the dolls. In addition to painting the dolls, artisans add natural objects such as shells, leather, fur, and feathers to decorate the dolls and establish their unique kachina identities.

Getting Started

Place newspapers on tables and prepare the work space for painting. Have students wear smocks for this project. Point out northeastern Arizona on a map and review the above information with students. Show them photographs of kachina dolls. Then demonstrate the steps as students follow along.

Materials

* photographs of kachina dolls
* small wood pieces in various shapes and sizes (such as cubes and cylinders)
* glue
* glue gun (optional, for adult use only)
* white, black, brown, red, yellow, and blue tempera paints
* paintbrushes
* water containers
* markers
* beads
* fabric and leather scraps
* scissors

Sensitivity Note

This project connects to a topic with deep spiritual significance for native cultures, including the Hopi. Please impress upon your students that the project is intended to help them learn about these cultures and develop respect and appreciation for them.

Resources

For Teachers

Easy Make & Learn Projects: Southwest Indians by Donald M. Silver and Patricia J. Wynne (Scholastic, 2005). Includes paper models and lessons to teach about Native American peoples of the Southwest, including the Hopi.

Following the Sun and the Moon: Hopi Kachina Tradition by Alph H. Secakuku (Northland, 1995). Written by a Hopi, this book explores the Hopi kachina ceremonial calendar.

Hopi Kachina Dolls: With a Key to Their Identification by Harold S. Colton (University of New Mexico Press, 1971). Written for collectors, the author describes the nuances that differentiate similar kachina dolls from one another.

Hopi Kachinas: The Complete Guide to Collecting Kachina Dolls by Barton Wright (Northland, 1977). A collector's guide to kachina dolls.

If You Lived With the Hopi Indians by Anne Kamma (Scholastic, 1999). In this book for older students, information about the Hopi is provided in a question-and-answer format.

For Students

Hopi by Barbara A. Gray-Kanatiiosh (Checkerboard Books, 2002). Easy-to-read text, along with photos and illustrations, provides an introduction to the Hopi people.

Is My Friend at Home? Pueblo Fireside Tales by John Bierhorst (Farrar, Straus and Giroux, 2001). Features seven retellings of traditional Hopi tales accompanied by lively illustrations.

Life in a Hopi Village (Picture the Past) by Sally Senzell Isaacs (Heinemann, 2000). The format of this nonfiction book helps students access information easily.

Directions

1 Practice arranging wood pieces to form a human shape. Small shapes work well for the head, legs, and arms. After selecting a balanced position of shapes, glue the pieces together and let dry.

2 Paint the doll with earth colors. (Mix paints as needed.) Encourage students to think about patterns and designs found in nature to use as inspiration as they decorate their dolls. Let dry.

3 Use markers to add small details for the face. Use simple geometric shapes to suggest eyes and other facial features.

4 Glue beads, fabric scraps, or leather scraps for added details. (If using a glue gun, an adult should complete this step.)

More Ideas

❖ Have students draw a portrait of their doll.

❖ Create a doll molded out of clay.

❖ Invite students to research other Hopi traditions.

References

Aboriginal Art of Australia: Exploring Cultural Traditions by Carol Finley (Lerner, 1999).

The African Cats by Geoffrey C. Saign (Franklin Watts, 1999).

African Fabrics: Sewing Contemporary Fashion With Ethnic Flair by Ronke Luke-Boone (Krause, 2001).

African Masks by Iris Hahner-Herzog (Prestel, 1998).

The American Quilt: A History of Cloth and Comfort 1750–1950 by Roderick Kiracofe (Clarkson Potter, 2004).

Ancient Egypt by Andrew Haslam (Two-Can Publishing, 2000).

Art From Many Hands: Multicultural Art Projects by Jo Miles Schuman (Davis, 2003).

The Art of African Masks: Exploring Cultural Traditions by Carol Finley (Lerner, 1999).

Brown Bag Ideas From Many Cultures by Irene Tejada (Davis, 1993).

Can You Spot the Leopard? African Masks by Christine Stelzig (Prestel, 1997).

Caribbean Elegance by Michael Connors and Bruce Buck (Harry N. Abrams, 2002).

Caribbean Style by Suzanne Slesin et al. (Three Rivers Press, 1998).

Cat Mummies by Kelly Trumble (Clarion, 1996).

The Cave of Lascaux by Mario Ruspoli (Harry N. Abrams, 1987).

The Chinese New Year's Dragon by Rachel Sing (Aladdin Paperbacks, 1994).

Classic Mosaic: Designs and Projects Inspired by 6,000 Years of Mosaic Art by Elaine M. Goodwin (Trafalgar Square, 2000).

Crafts of Many Cultures by Aurelia Gomez (Scholastic, 1992).

Culture Smart by Susan Rodriguez (Prentice Hall, 1999).

The Dancing Dragon by Marcia K. Vaughan (Mondo, 1996).

Dawn of Art: The Chauvet Cave by Eliette Brunel Deschamps (Harry N. Abrams, 1996).

Decorating Eggs: Exquisite Designs With Wax and Dye by Jane Pollak (Sterling, 1996).

The Dragon New Year: A Chinese Legend by David Bouchard (Peachtree, 1999).

Draw Rain Forest Animals by D. C. Dubosque (Peel Productions, 1994).

Eggs Beautiful: How to Make Ukrainian Easter Eggs by Johanna Luciow (Ukrainian Gift Shop, 1975).

The Egyptians by Joanna De Frates (Peter Bedrick, 2001).

Elephants by Norma S. Barrett (Scholastic, 1991).

Fabric (Craft Workshop) by Monica Stoppleman and Carol Crowe (Crabtree Publishing, 1998).

Flashy, Fantastic Rain Forest Frogs by Dorothy Hinshaw (Walker, 1999).

Following the Sun and the Moon: Hopi Kachina Tradition by Alph H. Secakuku (Northland, 1995).

Global Art by MaryAnn Kohl and Jean Potter (Gryphon House, 1998).

Great American Quilts by Sandra L. O'Brien
(Oxmor House, 1993).

The Great Kapok Tree: A Tale of the Amazon Rain Forest
by Lynne Cherry (Gulliver, 1990).

Hands-On Culture of West Africa by Kate O'Halloran
(J. Weston Walch, 1997).

Here Is the Tropical Rain Forest by Madeleine
Dunphy (Hyperion, 1997).

Hopi Kachina Dolls: With a Key to Their Identification
by Harold S. Colton (University of New
Mexico Press, 1971).

*Hopi Kachinas: The Complete Guide to Collecting Kachina
Dolls* by Barton Wright (Northland, 1977).

*Japan: A Portrait of the Country Through Its Festivals
and Traditions* (Fiesta) (Grolier, 1997).

Japanese Ink Painting: The Art of Sumi-e
by Naomi Okamoto (Sterling, 1996).

Japanese Ink Painting: Beginner's Guide to Sumi-E
by Susan Frame (Sterling, 2002).

Kente Colors by Deborah M. Newton Chocolate
(Walker Books for Young Readers, 1997).

The Last Dragon by Susan Miho Nunes
(Clarion Books, 1997).

Latin American Arts and Cultures by Dorothy Chaplik
(Davis, 2001).

Leif the Lucky by Ingri D'Aulaire
(Beautiful Fleet Books, 1995).

Lion Dancer: Ernie Wan's Chinese New Year
by Kate Waters (Scholastic, 1991).

Look Closer: Rain Forest by Barbara Taylor
(DK, 1998).

Making Mosaics: Designs, Techniques, and Projects
by Leslie Dierks (Sterling, 1997).

Masks of Black Africa by Ladislas Segy
(Dover, 1975).

Mediterranean Mosaic Designs by Anita Benarde
(Stemmer House, 1984).

Ms. Frizzle's Adventures: Ancient Egypt by Joanna Cole
(Scholastic, 2001).

Nature's Green Umbrella: Tropical Rain Forests
by Gail Gibbons (Harper, 1997).

Painters of the Caves by Patricia Lauber
(National Geographic, 1998).

Paper (Craft Workshop) by Helen Bliss
(Crabtree, 1998).

Printing: Arts & Crafts Skill by Susan Niner Janes
(Sea to Sea, 2005).

Rain Forest Birds (Birds Close Up) by Bobbie
Kalman and Barbara Bedell (Crabtree, 1998).

Rechenka's Eggs by Patricia Polacco
(Philomel, 1988).

*Rockin' Rain Sticks and Other Music Activities for
Elementary Children* by Linda Ray Miller
(Abingdon Press, 2002).

The Time of the Lion by Caroline Pitcher
(Beyond Words, 1998).

Tree Frogs (Animals of the Rain Forest)
by Erika Deiters and Jim Deiters
(Raintree/Steck Vaughn, 2000).

Ukrainian Egg Decoration: A Holiday Tradition
by Ann Stalcup (Powerkids Press, 1999).

The Vikings by Robert Livesay
(Stoddart Publishing, 1989).

The Vikings by Hazel Mary Martell and Henry
M. Martell (McGraw Hill, 1992).

The Weekend Crafter: Mosaics by Martin Cheek
(Lark Books, 1997).

Windmills and Wooden Shoes by Crystal Bowman
(Cygnet, 1999).